SpiritLife

FEED THE
CREATIVE FIRE

www.spiritlifepublishing.com
www.studythebiblenow.com

Root texts using in preparing these personal declarations include:

Seated In Heaven
The Book Of Ephesians Made Into A Personal Declaration Of God's Word

© 2015 David Lee Martin

For more information visit Davidleemartin.net
The Spirit Online Life Bible School
StudyTheBibleNow.com

Introduction

What you hold in your hands right now is not a book - it is a sword.

At least, that is what it is intended to be.

´When put to its intended use, you will know that it is not a book merely to be *read* - it is a book to be *said*!

The Scriptures tell us that God's Word is a spiritual sword - it is a sword that the Holy Spirit wields on our behalf, energising our life with divine life and power.

"For the Word that God speaks is alive and full of power [making it active, operative, energizing, and effective]; it is sharper than any two-edged sword, penetrating to the dividing line of the breath of life (soul) and [the immortal] spirit, and of joints and marrow [of the deepest parts of our nature], exposing and sifting and analyzing and judging the very thoughts and purposes of the heart." Hebrews 4:12 AMPLIFIED

"…and [take] the sword that the Spirit wields, which is the Word of God." Ephesians 6:17 AMPLIFIED

But to become a powerful weapon in the spiritual world, something important has to happen.

Using another military term, we could say that is not enough to load the gun - you have to pull the trigger to release the explosive potential that lies within.

That is what it is like with the Word of God.

We load our heart by hearing, reading

and meditating on the Word of God, but to unleash it's power we have to speak it out of our mouth!

A sword in its sheath is one thing, but it comes into its true purpose when it is unsheathed and wielded skilfully in the hand of a warrior.

You are a warrior, called and armed with spiritual weapons to pull down strongholds of the devil, and establish the Kingdom purposes of God.

This series of books is designed to help you do that.

Each book in the series includes a study on the power of words, directly from the rich teachings of the Scriptures.

The second part of each book then takes an individual letter or portion of the Scriptures and makes His Word, Your Word!

It is designed to be read aloud, from your

heart - filling your mouth with powerful truths that will seed your future with God's power and purpose for your life, your family, and your ministry.

I have intentionally made the text size of the second part of each book large. I want it to be as easy to read and proclaim for you as possible.

As you read through these strong, deep, Biblical confessions, over and over, you will internalise the truths that you hear yourself speaking. God's agreement from Heaven will establish in your life what you are speaking forth in the earth.

This, my friend, is the most powerful practice you can every engage in. It will change your life.

The Benefits of Applying the Word

"Wherefore lay apart all filthiness and superfluity of naughtiness, and receive with meekness the engrafted word, which is able to save your souls.

But be ye doers of the word, and not hearers only, deceiving your own selves.

For if any be a hearer of the word, and not a doer, he is like unto a man beholding his natural face in a glass:

For he beholdeth himself, and goeth his way, and straightway forgetteth what manner of man he was.

But whoso looketh into the perfect law of liberty, and continueth therein, he being not a forgetful hearer, but a doer of the work, this man shall be blessed in his deed.

If any man among you seem to be religious, and bridleth not his tongue, but deceiveth his own heart, this man's religion is vain." James 1:21-26 KJV

As with several of my other books, this one is intended to be applied. It's words and message are impotent if they are not vigorously applied.

As we can see from James stern warnings, merely reading or agreeing with a doctrine, does not transform our experience. It is acting upon the Truth that commands a blessing.

In verse 21 he encourages us to receive with meekness the engrafted Word. The Amplified translation expands on this idea, picturing the Word of God as a living seed that we plant and tend in our inner man:

"...in a humble (gentle, modest) spirit receive and welcome the Word which

implanted and rooted [in your hearts]
contains the power to save your souls." James
1:21 AMPLIFIED

Interestingly, verse 26 gives clear direction
how we can do this; bridling our tongue.

The 'His Word My Word' series of books
are a bridle that will train your tongue by
planting the Word in your heart, and harnessing
your testimony (the confession of your mouth)
with the glorious law of liberty - the perfect
Word of our Father.

Just a few the benefits you can expect as
you act on what you read, and become a doer of
the work include:

- It renews the mind, building into your
  consciousness and expectation new truths
  to live by.
- It moulds your vocabulary, harnessing
  your tongue to speak only those things
  God (and you) desire for your life.
- It conforms your thoughts and words to
  His thoughts and Words.

7

- It gives expression to the mind of Christ in any and all situations.
- It raises our perspective from earthly to heavenly, from below circumstances to above them.
- It banishes wrong thinking and emotions, replacing them with God's own thoughts - our emotions will always follow our thinking, and our thinking will follow the deposit in our heart, and the words of our mouths.
- It gives you an actionable principle you can apply to combat any adversity you face with confidence.
- It establishes Godly boundaries in your life.
- It overcomes the devil's plans and purposes because you are never in agreement with him, and they cannot be established.
- It develops new pictures of ourselves, ones that are shaped by God's unchanging love for us.
- It equips us with the necessary weapons for the Holy Spirit to bring to our remembrance what is needed to

overcome, any time our mind, body or spirit come under attack.

- It brings every thought into captivity and conformity to Christ, resulting in increased spiritual authority in the spirit realm and in relationships and ministry.
- It is health to our flesh and strength to our bones.

There are many more wonderful benefits that flow from disciplining ourselves to speak the Word only, but I am sure that you already you agree, any investment we need to make putting this into practice is far outweighed by the promised returns.

It is truly life changing, and a spiritual principle that will stand the test of time and every challenge that is thrown at it.

The Power Of Life And Death

As a Bible School teacher and developer of the Spirt Life Bible School (www.studythebiblenow.com), I am no stranger to the broad range of doctrines that we need to have a solid grasp of. There are some foundational truths that I come back to again and again however because they are truths that affect our every breath.

The most powerful of these is what the Bible says about the power of the words that we speak.

I am going come at this from several different angles, and I am certain that you will quickly see that this is not some side teaching of the Scriptures. It is a central strand of the

Christian life, the nervous system of the life of faith.

Whose Word Do You Trust?

Whenever I ask this question to a congregation of believers, I get several answers. Not surprisingly, the most popular are God, Jesus or The Holy Spirit. But the most honest answer hits home far more painfully than we would often like to admit. The word that has the greatest influence in your life is not necessarily God's (although it can be) - it is your own!

The words that proceed from your own lips are the ones you listen to, and the ones that you act upon.

How do I know this?

The Scriptures tell me that 'from the abundance of the heart the mouth speaks' (Matthew 12:34; Luke 6:45). Elsewhere we read that it is 'with the heart that man believes' (Romans 10:10).

The words that spill from our mouths locate what we really believe in our heart. And it is what we really believe in our heart that ultimately shapes our perception of reality. Many people believe, falsely, that there is no God. Now, the reality is that God not only exists, but has made Himself available to us in a very personal way. Such people will never know or state this life changing reality if their erroneous beliefs are not addressed.

But what of you and I? We are believers, but the facts will probably bear testimony that we still have many areas of our thoughts and beliefs that must be aligned with the glorious promises of Scripture.

There is often a gulf between our circumstances (the facts) and what God has promised (the reality and the truth).

The question for us is who do we bridge that gap?

I think I have the answer for you, and thankfully it is one that you can put into motion within the next 10 seconds: the way to bring the facts and circumstances of your existence closer to the promises of God is through your intentional use of words.

Again, looking in Romans chapter 10, the Holy Spirit writes;

"…with the mouth confession is made unto salvation."

That tiny word 'unto' denotes 'entrance into' and 'moving towards'.

For us to 'enter into' and 'move toward' the reality of God's promises being manifest in our life, we must activate both of the faculties of the faith life: a heart that believes the promises of God, and a mouth that speaks forth those promises, giving breath to them.

F.F. Bosworth, author of the classic 'Christ the Healer' wrote, "The Word is lifeless until faith is breathed into it on your lips. Then it becomes a supernatural force."

Read those words carefully one more time.

If you want God's Word to become a supernatural force in your life, rather than just a desirable doctrine, life must be breathed upon it through your own lips.

If I truly want God's Word to take first place in my life, it must first become My Word!

Engaging With Jesus Today

This, to me, is one of the most profound points of doctrine that we can grasp.

We hear much about the life of Jesus. But He is no longer walking the dusty shores of Galilee.

We have sermons galore about the cross, and the glorious results of the sacrifice that Jesus made. But, thank God, Jesus is no longer on the cross. For us to follow Him we must take leave of the cross and head on toward the resurrection.

Peering into the tomb we still do not find our Lord. The angel plainly asks, "Why are you looking for the living among the dead? He is not here."

Running to the mount, maybe we will find Him speaking of the Kingdom and His glory?

Even here, our Lord is absent. Maybe we could join the small band of disciples staring up into the clouds, mouths agape in amazement. But again, God soon sends His angels to move us on.

So where do we go to engage with Jesus Christ and His present day ministry?

We must operate from a higher place, one where we are seated together with Him in heavenly places.

And how do we do this?

It should come as no surprise that the answer is, through the words that you choose to speak.

The High Priest Of Our Confession

Let me begin this short exposition with a few verses to set the stage…

"Now the main point of what we have to say is this: We have such a High Priest, One Who is seated at the right hand of the majestic [God] in heaven…" Hebrews 8:1 AMPLIFIED

"Wherefore, holy brethren, partakers of the heavenly calling, consider the Apostle and High Priest of our profession, Christ Jesus;" Hebrews 3:1 KJV

"Seeing then that we have a great High Priest who has passed through the heavens, Jesus the Son of God, let us hold fast our confession." Hebrews 4:14 NKJV

Here Paul says that the sum of all he had said to the Hebrews was this one truth - we have a High Priest in Heaven. This, he stressed, was the main point his readers needed to grasp.

And it something we need to grasp too.

Knowing how to effectively engage with Jesus present day ministry is essential for our progress. Thankfully, these verses also make the mode of operation very clear - He is the High Priest of our 'confession'.

He releases His authority and blessing in proportion to the release of our confession. The two things are intimately connected.

Of course, it should also be noted that negative words, and words that are not in agreement with what God has already said over our lives, not only nullify the ability of God to intervene, it plays directly into the hands of negative forces, who seize upon those wrong words and use them aggressively against us, and against God's purposes being worked out in our lives.

Say The Same Thing As

Digging a little deeper we can even more accurately understand what is being said in these verses concerning the High Priestly ministry of Jesus on our behalf.

To do that we need to take a look beneath the text at the original Greek, particularly at the word translated 'confession' (or 'profession' in some versions).

The word is homologia (Strongs #3671) (homologia from homoú = together with + légo = say)

It literally means "To say the same thing as", Or "to say together with".

And who are we to say the same thing as? God of course, and His Words as recorded in the Scriptures. This, my friend, is where the power of transformation and miracles in your life resides.

When we align our words with His, we receive the full backing of Jesus, our High Priest.

This is not some hocus-pocus new age technique. We cannot just pull a fanciful desire out of the air and begin saying over and over again, "I win the lottery, I win the lottery".

The spirit of faith does not work in an arbitrary way. There are clear guidelines and spiritual principles, which, when understood and put into effect, bring God on the scene and give Him permission to act on our behalf and accomplish the impossible.

In the next section, I am going to pull these guidelines apart so we can eat the meat of them together and see how we might apply them in our lives today.

The Power Of Life And Death

"Death and life are in the power of the tongue, and they who indulge in it shall eat the fruit of it [for death or life]."
Proverbs 18:21

It is a sobering thought to realise that every word that proceeds from your mouth is a seed that will one day grow up, and whose fruit you will eat. Essentially, this means that you are eating today what you planted yesterday, and you will taste tomorrow what you plant today.

The question you need to ask yourself is this, am I planting the kind of life I want I want to experience in my future, or am I planting death? The power for both is right now in your tongue.

Jesus spoke of this again and again. Some of the most quoted verses are found in Mark chapter 11.

"So Jesus answered and said to them, "Have faith in God.

For assuredly, I say to you, whoever says to this mountain, "Be removed and be cast into the sea,' and does not doubt in his heart, but believes that those things he says will be done, he will have whatever he says.

Therefore I say to you, whatever things you ask when you pray, believe that you receive them, and you will have them." Mark 11:22-24 NKJV

I want you to notice a few things here.

Number one, we are told to have faith in God. These words can also be rendered, "have the faith of God". In fact, this is precisely how God Himself works - He speaks from the rich deposit in His heart, and it springs into being. From the very first verses of Genesis, this is shown to be His mode of operation. We are encouraged, as those created in His image and endued with the supernatural faculty of language, to do the same.

Secondly, take a look at how many times Jesus emphasises the power of words -

"For assuredly, I say to you, whoever

says to this mountain, "Be removed and be cast into the sea,' and does not doubt in his heart, but believes that those things he says will be done, he will have whatever he says."

Consider the final statement here, "he will have whatever he says".

You will have whatever you say!

Speak To The Mountain,
Not About The Mountain

A third and very pertinent point is that Jesus told us to speak to the mountain, not about the mountain.

A mountain is something that refuses to be ignored. It stands in our way, an obstacle to our path. At times, it will insist that it is insurmountable, impossible to conquer.

The temptation is to agree with the testimony of that mountainous problem or circumstance and speak about it with everyone we meet. We talk and gossip about how terrible our problem is: how this sickness is killing us, or how the bills are piling up and we do not have the means to pay them.

Jesus told us to say one thing to these mountains - "Be Removed!"

Our testimony will either agree with the problem or the solution. You can either perpetuate the problem by speaking it over and over again, or you can annihilate the problem by speaking the solution as found in the Word of God.

And we are not just talking about obstacles outside of ourselves. Sometimes they are easier to deal with, and it is the deep rooted issues that keep us bound to old ways and patterns.

The same solution applies to both.

"And the Lord said, If ye had faith as a grain of mustard seed, ye might say unto this sycamine tree, Be thou plucked up by the root, and be thou planted in the sea; and it should obey you." Luke 17:6 KJV

Even deep-rooted obstacles can be dealt with through intentional words of faith spoken from the heart.

Do You Say What You Have
or Do You Have What You Say?

Finally, Jesus did not tell us to "say what we have". He said that we would "have what we say". These are two very different propositions.

Too often we spend all of our energy and attention saying what we have (or do not have!) rather than spending that same breath on establishing those things that we want based on God's promises.

Scripture tells us that it is through agreement and decree that we establish a thing.

"Thou shalt also decree a thing, and it shall be established unto thee: and the light shall shine upon thy ways." Job 22:28

"...at the mouth of two witnesses, or at the mouth of three witnesses, shall the matter be established." Deuteronomy 19:15

Let God's Word be the first witness in any matter, and let your lips be the second establishing witness. As you put His Word on your lips Heaven and Earth agree, and power is released to affect change in the situation you are addressing.

Righteousness Has A Voice

Coming back again to Romans 10, the Holy Spirit not only tells us that righteousness has a voice, He also tells us how right standing with God will speak.

Let's turn there again, and unpack and apply this truth.

The portion of Scripture we are referring to is Romans 10:6-11.

"But the righteousness which is of faith speaketh on this wise, Say not in thine heart, Who shall ascend into heaven? (that is, to bring Christ down from above:)

Or, Who shall descend into the deep? (that is, to bring up Christ again from the dead.)

But what saith it? The word is nigh thee, even in thy mouth, and in thy heart: that is, the word of faith, which we preach;

That if thou shalt confess with thy mouth the Lord Jesus, and shalt believe in thine heart that God hath raised him from the dead, thou shalt be saved.

For with the heart man believeth unto righteousness; and with the mouth confession is made unto salvation.

For the scripture saith, Whosoever believeth on him shall not be ashamed." (Romans 10:6-11 KJV)

Right standing with God, as received through faith in Jesus Christ, is yours right now. And this privileged position and understand that we have as believers should shape how we speak.

Paul makes it clear that a proper understanding of our position in Christ does NOT say, "Jesus, come down". How often have we heard, or even prayed this way ourselves? "Come Lord Jesus, Come down in our midst, come into this or that circumstance"?

But the Scriptures here teach us a better way, an unfailing avenue to usher God's presence and power into any situation.

Paul also tells us that righteousness does not say, "Jesus, come up!"

I guess this refers to the kind of sentiment that laments, "If only Jesus were here now, if only He could touch me" and so on.

So righteousness (and according to 2 Corinthians 5:21 you are the righteousness of God in Christ Jesus) does not say, "Jesus, come down" or "Jesus, come up".

What does it say?

Righteousness says, "Jesus is right here, right now - in my heart and in my mouth!"

How? Through the Word.

Jesus and the Word of God are one.

As Solomon says in Ecclesiastes 8:4:

"Where the word of a king is, there is power..."

When we speak the Word, we immediately connect with His authority, and His

High Priestly ministry and bring His victory to bear upon any situation or circumstance we speak into.

Words Become Things

"O generation of vipers, how can ye, being evil, speak good things? for out of the abundance of the heart the mouth speaketh.

A good man out of the good treasure of the heart bringeth forth good things: and an evil man out of the evil treasure bringeth forth evil things." (Matthew 12:34 KJV)

Again we see the close relationship the Bible ascribes between the heart and the lips - the words that we speak.

Whatever your heart is full of, your mouth will speak.

Your heart is like the soil that receives whatever words are planted in it, for good or for bad. And like any seed that is sown, it grows up and multiplies. It brings forth fruit.

Jesus here describes this process and explains that from the heart the mouth will speak, and bring things forth!

What is invisible and intangible, becomes visible as it is spoken consistently into existence from the heart.

The system is a lot like the water cycle - words are deposited in the heart through hearing them spoken, the heart is filled and overflows and the mouth speaks from the heart's abundance - the words that are spoken from the heart are heard by the ears and deposited in the heart, and so on.

The Holy Spirit alludes to this picture in Isaiah 11:

""For My thoughts are not your thoughts, Nor are your ways My ways," says the LORD.
"For as the heavens are higher than the earth, So are My ways higher than your ways, And My thoughts than your thoughts.
"For as the rain comes down, and the snow from heaven, And do not return there, But water the earth, And make it bring forth and bud, That it may give seed to the sower And bread to the eater,

So shall My word be that goes forth from My mouth; It shall not return to Me void, But it shall accomplish what I please, And it shall prosper in the thing for which I sent it." Isaiah 55:8 NKJV

Do note that it is "that goes forth from My mouth" that accomplishes what it pleases, and prospers in the thing for which you send it.

What words are you sending out to accomplish for you today?

The determiner is what we choose to put into our heart and allow to be spoken from our mouth.

Luke 8:11 says that words are seeds. The fruit we eat and enjoy in life will be absolutely determined by the seed that we sow.

God's Words are life and health.

"My son, attend to my words; incline thine ear unto my sayings.
Let them not depart from thine eyes;

keep them in the midst of thine heart.

For they are life unto those that find them, and health to all their flesh.

Keep thy heart with all diligence; for out of it are the issues of life.

Put away from thee a froward mouth, and perverse lips put far from thee." Proverbs 4:20-24

Notice the cycle - attend to God's Word by inclining your ear to hear them. Through your eyes and ears deposit the God's Words in your heart, filling your spirit with life and health. Then, as you keep and fill your heart in this way, it will issue forth life, and wrong speaking will be put away from you. Your mouth will minister words of life, which in turn will continue the cycle of life-giving, fruit-bearing, supernatural living.

You Are The Prophet Of Your Own Life

At times, we can think that the words from someone else's mouth are more powerful than your own. We can hunt for words from the mouth of some great preacher or a prophecy from another renowned prophet. But, believe me, as powerful and life-changing as those words may be, they are nothing in comparison to the words that you hear spoken from your own mouth.

And when you fill your heart and mouth with God's perfect Word, His spiritual life-cycle will go to work in your life to refresh, strengthen, change, transform, and make fruitful every area of your life.

As you do, you set the rudder of your life to carry you to the destination God has prescribed for you.

Read chapter 3 of James and you will see just how important this is.

The entire chapter is packed with

revelation, but let's just focus in on a few verses.

"For we all often stumble and fall and offend in many things. And if anyone does not offend in speech [never says the wrong things], he is a fully developed character and a perfect man, able to control his whole body and to curb his entire nature.

If we set bits in the horses' mouths to make them obey us, we can turn their whole bodies about.

Likewise, look at the ships: though they are so great and are driven by rough winds, they are steered by a very small rudder wherever the impulse of the helmsman determines. Even so is the tongue is a little member..." James 3:2-5

Your tongue is the rudder of your life.

If you are not heading in the direction you want, you need to change the words that you are speaking.

And as with any ocean voyage, your life will face tremendous challenges and storms at times. It is at these times the winds and the waves will pull and tug at your ship, goading you to weaken your grip and yield to their pressure - in our case say things contrary to the direction and destination set before us in the Word of God.

For this reason, it is essential that you strengthen your spiritual muscles when the seas are open, and the sailing is plain. Don't wait for the storms before you learn to steer your ship and tame your tongue (with God's help and guidance). As you confess God's Word it will shape your speaking, and when the hard times come your rudder will be set, and uncompromising.

Walking By Faith

I think by now we have established that this principle is found throughout the New Testament.

Paul says we are to "walk by faith, not by sight" (2 Corinthians 5:7).

But how do we do that? What does the Bible teach about walking by faith, and what's the problem with walking by sight?

These are questions I asked the Holy Spirit myself, and His answer is plain and simple.

Sometimes people want to spiritualise things so much, make them so mysterious, that ordinary folk like you and I feel that they are out of reach. That is not how the Holy Spirit works.

Anyone close to me knows that I believe in encounters with God, in visions and dreams, and all of the supernatural manifestations of God's presence and gifts as seen in the Bible, and I believe that they are for today, not relegated to obscurity by some dispensational doctrine that says that they passed away.

But all of these things are not how we walk by faith. We do not need a vision or a dream. We don't even need a dramatic encounter or to fast, pray and speak in tongues for several hours a day, to walk by faith.

Walking by faith according to the Bible, is so simple that any one who chooses to, can apply it every day of their life and in every situation they face.

"We having the same spirit of faith, according as it is written, I believed, and therefore have I spoken; we also believe, and therefore speak;"   2 Corinthians 4:13

The spirit of faith does two things: believes and speaks.

To walk by faith is to walk by your believing and your speaking. That's it. It really is that simple.

Hebrews 11:1-3 teaches that faith gives substance to the things that we hope for. It pulls the invisible unrealities of hope, and gives substance to them. Our world is framed by His Word, and our faith is released to accomplish His will as we release His Word from our mouths.

The word translated 'framed' here is Strongs #2675 Katartizó.

It carries the idea of completion, preparation of true purpose, destination or use, bring into its proper condition (whether for the first time, or after a lapse), adjust to be in good order, to fully function - to equip, fully train, to make thoroughly complete, mend (what has been broken or rent) or restore.

Hebrews 11:1 also contains another powerful key; "Now" faith is…

Faith calls those things that are not yet, as if they are already so (Romans 4:17). When faith prays, it believes that it receives NOW those things it prays for (Mark 11:24).

The weak do not look at their weakness, instead, despite what they see, they say that they are strong (Joel 3:10).

When Jesus spoke, He did not do so to merely give us information - His Words were spoken to release the power and potential of Heaven in the earth. Every Word is pregnant with God's power, and we are invited to take hold of those Words, receive them in our heart, and experience them for ourselves. His Word is a creative force.

The key is to receive them for yourself. All of God's promises are "Yes!" in Christ Jesus, are you going to add your "Amen"?

"For all the promises of God in Him are Yes, and in Him Amen, to the glory of God through us." 2 Corinthians 1:20

I believe we bring our agreement, our "Amen", by personalising the promises of God as given through Christ, and speaking them out as if (and they are) already ours.

I think you can see easily how powerful this is in relation to our own lives.

Don't Dissect The Bible

I am a big fan of systematic theology - formulating Biblical teaching on different subjects so we can get a proper understanding. The problem is, in seeking to rightly divide the Word of truth, we sometimes dissect things and miss the broader holistic message and testimony originally intended.

For years, my wife and I have taken the New Testament Scriptures relating to what is said about who we are 'in Christ' and made them our confession. And this is a powerful practice. What struck me recently though, is that the New Testament was not written split into chapter and verse. The letters were written as a complete thought, and in between our favourite verses to quote and claim, there is a wealth of life that God wants to establish in our lives.

It led me on a fresh and wonderful journey, revisiting the letters of the New Testament, and personalising them - applying them to my own life and confession. Taking those words, as spoken by the Holy Ghost, and making them my own. In line with the encouragement of Hebrews to 'hold fast my confession', and 'say the same thing as' Jesus has already spoken over my life as a redeemed child of God.

His Word My Word

Not only does this process of combing God's Word to personalise its message, and then actively, intentionally, and consistently confessing that Word, radically change your thinking and the way you perceive the world, it also plants that Word deep in your heart. When challenges come, without thinking, the solution will be brought to your remembrance, and a sword of truth will immediately arise from the abundance of your heart to combat all that is contrary to God's will and purpose in your life.

My heartfelt prayer is that you will take the words on the following pages of this book, and make them your own. Aggressively fill your mouth with these powerful truths taken directly from God's own Word, and watch as they accomplish the miracles they were sent to bring into being when the breath of life is breathed upon them on your lips.

The Book Of Ephesians made Into A Personal Declaration Of God's Word

The book of Ephesians is one of the richest resources for the saint of God. Paul's letter contains so much insight to our present position and privileges in Christ Jesus.

Declaring these realities boldly from our mouth is life-changing.

Take the words on the following pages, salt them with your own thanksgiving, and rise up to take your place in God's affections and authority.

[Speak aloud and with confidence. These are God's promises given to you in Christ Jesus. They belong to you today.]

"God's Word is true for me today.

I am who the Bible says I am.

I have what the Bible says I have.

His Word is true, and I believe in my heart and confess with my mouth that Jesus is Lord of every aspect of my life.

As I make these declarations directly from the Word of God, I release faith, and they prosper in that for which they were sent."

I am a saint…

I am a saint, consecrated and set apart by God.

I'm faithful, loyal and steadfast in Christ Jesus.

God's grace, unmerited favour, and spiritual peace, are mine. I live in harmony, unity and undisturbedness.

I am blessed in Christ Jesus with every spiritual blessing in the heavenly realm.

In his love, God chose me, actually picked me out for himself as his own. He chose me in Christ before the foundation of the world that I should be holy, consecrated and set apart for him.

I am blameless in his sight, above reproach, and I stand before him in love. He foreordained, destined and planned in love for me to be adopted and revealed as his own child through Christ. And he did this according to his own will because it pleased him and was his kind intent.

My life commends his glorious grace, favour, and mercy, to others, a grace that is freely bestowed upon me in his beloved Son, Jesus.

I am redeemed…

I have redemption through his blood – complete deliverance, and complete salvation.

All of my sins are forgiven, every offense, shortcoming and trespass is remitted.

I enjoy the riches and generosity of his gracious favour over my life.

His Grace has been lavished upon me in every kind of wisdom and understanding, practical insight and prudence.

God makes known to me the mystery of his will, his plan, and his purposes.

All of this was God's good pleasure, already planned and set forth in Christ for me.

I am God's heritage and portion, and I have obtained an inheritance in him.

He foreordained that I should be chosen and appointed to live fully in his purpose, in complete agreement with the counsel and design of God's own perfect will.

I'm destined to live for the

praise of His glory.

I hear the word of truth, accept the good news of my salvation, and believe in and adhere to Jesus with my whole being.

I am sealed by the Spirit...

I am stamped with the seal of the Holy Spirit.

The Spirit is the absolute guarantee of my inheritance. He is the first fruits, the pledge and foretaste of good things to come – the anticipation of my full redemption and my acquiring complete possession of it – to the praise of his glory.

I do not cease to give thanks.

The God of our Lord Jesus Christ, the Father of glory, grants me the spirit of wisdom and revelation, insight into mysteries and secrets, in the deep and intimate knowledge of Him.

The eyes of my heart are flooded with light.

I know and understand the hope to which He is called me, and how rich is glorious inheritance is in the saints.

I know and understand the immeasurable and unlimited and surpassing greatness of his power in and for me because I truly believe.

I am a believer, not a doubter.

His mighty strength is demonstrated and works powerfully in and through me – the same power He exerted in Jesus Christ when he raised him from the dead and seated to Him at His own right hand in the heavenly places.

I am seated in Heaven…

I am seated with Christ, far above all rule and authority, all

power and dominion, and every
name that is named.

All things have been put under
His feet, and I am in him.

He is the head of my life, and
his fullness fills me – the full
measure of Him, who makes
everything complete, filling every
part of my life with Himself.

And I have been made alive,
who was once a dead in trespasses
and sins.

I am no longer dead in
trespasses and sins, and I no longer
walk in them.

I do not follow the course and fashion of this world.

I am not under the sway and tendency of this present age.

I do not follow the prince of the power of the air.

I'm not obedient to or under the control of any demon spirit.

I'm not disobedient, rebellious, careless or unbelieving.

I do not go against the purposes of God.

I do not live or conduct myself in the passions of my flesh.

My behaviour is not governed by a corrupt and sensual nature.

I do not obey the impulses of my flesh, or the thoughts of my mind – the cravings dictated by my senses and dark imaginings.

I am not under God's wrath because He is rich in mercy toward me!

He loves me with a great, wonderful, and intense love.

I am dead to sin and alive to

God...

Even when I was dead in sin, slain by my own shortcomings and trespasses, God the Father made me alive together with Christ.

I am alive in fellowship and union with Jesus, the Anointed One.

I have the very life of Christ Himself – the same new life which raised Jesus from the dead and made Him alive. This resurrection life is mine today!

By his undeserved grace, favour, and mercy, I am saved.

I am delivered from judgement.

I am a partaker of Christ's salvation.

I'm raised up together with Him, and I have been made to sit with Him in heavenly realms.

I'm seated right now in the Messiah, the anointed one.

God is now, and through the ages to come, demonstrating in me, the immeasurable, limitless, surpassing riches of his free grace – His unmerited favour, kindness, and goodness of heart toward me in

Christ Jesus.

By grace, I am saved through faith.

I am delivered from judgement, and I am a partaker of Christ's salvation.

My salvation is not of myself, not of my own doing, not a result of my own striving; it is the gift of God.

I receive the gift of salvation in every part of my life today.

My place of favour and blessing is not by works, not the

result of the fulfilment of any law, and what I could not possibly do for myself, He did for me.

I give God all the glory.

I walk and live in God's perfect plan for my life…

I am God's handiwork.

I am His workmanship, recreated in Christ Jesus, born anew so I might do those good works that He has predestined and planned beforehand for me.

I am taking paths which He has prepared for me ahead of time.

I walked completely in the paths, and in the works that He has prepared, living the good life that He has prearranged and made ready for me to live.

I am no longer separated from God.

I am no longer excluded.

I'm not a stranger to the covenants of God.

I have an eternal hope.

I am not without God in the world. He is my very own Father.

I've been brought near, by, in, and through the blood of Christ.

He Himself is my peace.

He is my bond of unity and harmony.

Every hostile, dividing wall has been broken down.

Through Jesus, I have access by the Holy Spirit to the Father, and I boldly approach God without fear or condemnation.

God lives in me, and I live in Him…

I am truly a citizen of God's kingdom.

I belong to God's own household.

Jesus is my cornerstone, and I stand upon the foundation of the apostles and the prophets.

I am built together with other believers, and we grow together and continue to rise as a holy temple in the Lord – a sanctuary dedicated, consecrated as sacred to the presence of the Lord.

In Him, and in fellowship with

others, I am being built up by the Spirit as a living temple for God himself.

God dwells in me.

I am an heir of God, and a joint-heir together with Jesus Christ.

I share in His divine promises.

I'm a minister of the gospel according to the free grace of God — bestowed on me by the exercise in all its effectiveness of His power.

I'm a recipient of the unending, boundless, fathomless, incalculable, and exhaustless riches of Christ — a wealth that no human being could ever have searched out!

Through me, the many-sided wisdom of God in all its infinite variety and innumerable aspects is made known to the angelic rulers and authorities in the heavenlies.

I have the boldness, courage, and confidence of free access – an unreserved approach to God with freedom and without fear.

I do not lose heart, faint or become despondent through fear.

God, out of the rich treasury of his glory, strengthens and reinforces me with mighty power in my inner man by the Holy Spirit.

God Himself indwells my innermost being and personality.

Through faith Christ dwells, settles down, and makes his permanent home in my heart.

I am rooted deep in love and founded securely on love.

I have power, and I'm strong to apprehend and grasp with all the saints the experience of that love; the breadth, length, height and depth of it.

I've come to know, practically and through experience for myself, the love of Christ, which far surpasses mere knowledge.

I am filled through my whole being unto all the fullness of God.

I have the richest measure of the divine presence, and I'm a body wholly filled and flooded with God Himself.

God's power is at work in me to do superabundantly, far over and above all that I dare ask or think – infinitely beyond my highest prayers, desires, hopes or dreams.

I walk and lead a life worthy of the divine calling to which I have been called.

I behave in a manner that is a credit to the summons to God's service.

I live with complete lowliness of mind and humility, with meekness, unselfishness, gentleness and mildness – with patience, bearing with others and making allowances because I love others as Christ loves me.

I am eager and strive to guard and keep the harmony and oneness produced by the Holy Spirit in the binding power of peace.

God is my Father, above all, pervading and living in me.

Grace has been given to me, in proportion to the measure of Christ's rich and bounteous gift.

His presence fills all things, the whole universe, from the lowest to the highest.

I am an effective minister of the gospel...

I am consecrated and equipped to do the work of the ministry, building up the body of Christ, till we all attain oneness in the faith, and in the comprehension of the full and accurate knowledge of the Son of God.

I arrive at really mature manhood – the completeness of personality which is nothing less than the standard height of Christ's own perfection – the measure of the stature of the fullness of Christ, and the completeness found in him.

I'm no longer a child, tossed to and fro between chance winds of doctrine.

Rather, my life lovingly expresses truth in all things.

I speak truly.

I deal truly.

I live truly.

Enfolded in love, I grow up in Him in every way – in all things I grow into Him, who is the Head – even Christ the Messiah, the Anointed One.

I'm closely joined and knit together with the body of Christ.

I work properly and function, growing to full maturity and building the body of Christ up in love.

I no longer live as the heathen do in perverseness, vanity and emptiness of soul, and in futility of mind.

My heart is not hard or insensitive. My conscience is not calloused.

I am taught by the Anointing.

I strip myself of my former nature. I put off and discard my old unrenewed self.

I'm constantly renewed in the spirit of my mind – having a fresh mental and spiritual attitude.

I put on the new nature, created in God's image, Godlike in true righteousness and holiness.

I reject all falsity, and I express truths with my neighbour.

I never let the sun go down on my wrath, exasperation, fury or indignation.

I do not leave any foothold for the devil, and I give no opportunity to him.

I do not steal, but I make an honest living with my own hands, so that I may be able to give to those in need.

I let no foul or polluting language, evil word or unwholesome or worthless talk, ever come out of my mouth.

My words are only good, and beneficial to the spiritual progress of others, giving grace and God's favour any who hear me.

I do not grieve the Holy Spirit. I do not vex, offend or sadden Him.

By the Holy Spirit, I was sealed, marked, and branded as God's own – secured for the day of redemption, my final deliverance through Christ from evil and the consequences of sin.

I banish all bitterness and indignation from my life.

I banish wrath, rage and bad temper.

I banish resentment, anger, animosity and quarrelling, brawling, clamour and contention from my life.

I banish slander, evil-speaking, abusive or blasphemous language of any kind.

All malice, spite and ill will, or baseness of any kind, is banished from my life.

I am useful, helpful and kind to others – tenderhearted, compassionate, understanding and loving hearted.

I forgive others readily and freely as Christ forgive me.

I am an imitator of God, I copy Him and followed His example, as a well-beloved child imitates their Father.

I walk in love, esteeming and delighting in others, just as Christ loves me and gave Himself up for me.

I forsake all immorality.

I forsake all sexual vice and impurity.

I forsake all lustful, rich, wasteful living, and all greediness.

I refuse and reject all filthiness from my life, all obscenity and indecency.

I let no foolish, sinful, silly or corrupt talk, nor coarse jesting, come from my lips.

Instead, I voiced my thankfulness to God.

I practice no sexual vice or impurity in thought or life.

I forsake all covetousness and idolatry.

I do not lust after the property of others, and I am not greedy for gain.

I have an inheritance in the kingdom of Christ and God.

I do not associate with the works, or the workers of darkness, rebellion or disobedience.

For I was once darkness, but now I am light in the Lord.

As a child of light, I walk in the light, as one native born to the light.

The fruit, affect, and product of the light in my life, consists in every form of kindness, goodness, uprightness of heart, and trueness of life.

I'm kind, good, upright and honest.

I learn by experience what is pleasing to the Lord.

My life is a constant proof and example of what is most acceptable to Him.

I take no part in and have no fellowship with, the unfruitful works of darkness.

Instead I live my life in a way that exposes, reproves and convicts them.

I am vitally awake and alive to God, risen from the dead.

Christ shines upon me and gives me light.

I look carefully how I walk, living purposefully, worthily and accurately – not as unwise and witless, but wisely, sensibly and intelligently.

I redeem the time, making the most of every opportunity because the days are evil.

I'm not vague, thoughtless or foolish.

I understand and firmly grasp what the will of the Lord is.

I do not get drunk with wine, which is debauchery, but I am ever filled with and stimulated with the

Holy Spirit.

I speak out in psalms, hymns, and spiritual songs, making melody with all of my heart to the Lord.

At all times and for everything I give thanks in the name of our Lord Jesus Christ to God my Father.

I'm submissive and humble in heart out of reverence for Christ.

- - - - - - - - - - - - - - - -

[WIVES]

I am submissive and adapt myself to my own husband as a

service to the Lord.

My husband is my head as
Christ is the head of the church, and
the Saviour of His body.

As the church is subject to
Christ, so I am subject in everything
to my husband.

My husband loves me as
Christ loves the church and gave
himself for her, so He might sanctify
her, having cleansed by the washing
of water with the word.

I'm presented to my husband
in glorious splendour, without sport
or wrinkle or any such thing.

I am holy and without fault.

My husband loves me as his own body, knowing that he who loves his wife loves himself.

My husband nourishes, carefully protects, and cherishes me, as Christ does the church.

I'm joined to my husband, and we are one flesh.

I respect and reverence my husband.

I notice him, regard him, honour him, prefer him, venerate

and esteem him, deferring to him, loving and admiring him exceedingly.

- - - - - - - - - - - - - - - -

[HUSBANDS]

My wife is subject to me, out of reverence for Christ. She is submissive and adapts herself to me as a service to the Lord.

I'm the head of my wife as Christ is the head of the church, Himself the saviour of the body.

As the church is subject to Christ, my wife is subject to me in everything.

I love my wife as Christ loves the church and gave Himself up for her.

I sanctify her, cleansing her by the washing of water with the word.

My wife is glorious, splendid, without spot or wrinkle. She is holy and faultless, and I love her exceedingly.

I love my wife as my own body, knowing that he who loves his wife loves himself.

I nourish, carefully protect, and

I cherish her as Christ does the church.

I've left my father and mother, and I'm joined to my wife. We are one flesh.

I love my wife as my very own self.

My wife respects and references me.

She notices me, regards me, honours me, prefers and venerates and esteems me.

She defers to me, praising me, loving me and admiring me

exceedingly.

- - - - - - - - - - - - - - - -

[PARENTS]

My children obey me in the Lord, as his representative, for this is just an right.

My children honour, esteem and value their parents as precious − fulfilling the first commandment with a promise.

It is well with my children, and they live long on the Earth.

- - - - - - - - - - - - - - - -

[CHILDREN]

I obey my parents in the Lord, as his representatives, but this is just and right.

I honour, esteem and value my parents as precious – fulfilling the first commandment with a promise.

Because of this, it is well with me, and I live long on the Earth.

- - - - - - - - - - - - - - - -

[FATHERS]

I do not irritate or provoke my

children to anger.

I do not exasperate them to resentment.

I rear my children in the training, discipline and the counsel and admonition of the Lord.

- - - - - - - - - - - - - - - -

[IN RESPECT TO AUTHORITY]

I'm obedient to those who are my superiors, having respect for them and eager concern to please them.

In singleness of motive and with all my heart I serve them as a service to Christ Himself.

In all things I do the will of God heartily and with my whole soul, not with eye service, but as a servant of Christ, rendering service readily, with goodwill, as to the Lord and not to men.

I know that whatever good I do, I will receive my reward from the Lord.

I never use threatening, violent or abusive words, knowing that my Master is in heaven and that there is no respect of persons with Him.

- - - - - - - - - - - - - - - -

I am strong with the strength of God…

I am strong in the Lord, empowered through my union with him.

I draw my strength from God, a strength that His boundless might provides.

I put on God's whole armour, the armour of heavy-armed soldier that God supplies.

I successfully stand up against

all the strategies and deceits of the devil, knowing that I do not wrestle with flesh and blood, or with physical opponents, but against powers, master spirits, world rulers of this present darkness, against the spiritual forces of wickedness in the heavenly supernatural sphere.

I put on God's complete armour.

I resist and stand my ground in the evil day of danger, and having done all the crisis demands, I stand firmly in my place.

I stand, holding my ground.

I tighten the belt of truth around my loins.

I put on the breastplate of integrity, moral rectitude, and right standing with God.

My feet are shod in preparation to face the enemy with firm-footed stability, with the promptness and readiness produced by the good news of the gospel of peace.

I lift up over all the shield of saving faith, upon which I can quench all the flaming missiles of the wicked one.

I take the helmet of salvation.
My thoughts are protected.

I take up the sword of the
spirit, the sword that the Holy Spirit
wields, which is the word of God.

I pray in the Spirit at all times,
on every occasion and in every
season, with all manner of prayer
and entreaty.

To that end, I keep alert and
watch with strong purpose and
perseverance, interceding in behalf of
all the saints - God's consecrated
people.

I have freedom of utterance,

and I open my mouth to proclaim boldly the mystery of the good news of the gospel.

I am an ambassador of the gospel, declaring it boldly and courageously.

My heart is consoled, cheerful, encouraged, and strengthened.

The peace of God is mine, with love and faith from the Father, and from the Lord Jesus Christ.

Today, I receive God's grace, his undeserved and unmerited favour.

I love my Lord Jesus Christ with an undying and incorruptible love.

Amen.

About The Author

David Lee Martin is a passionate and very imperfect Christian. Although he is an ordained pastor, and the author and administrator of the Spirit Life Online Bible School, he chooses to not put too much confidence in those things to shape his identity.

At the end of the day, he is very much like you, a man who has discovered that there really is a gracious God who has called us to know Him in a real and tangible way.

His life vocation is to discover more of the grace he has tasted, and to share it with others.

David is happily married to Larna, and they have four awesome kids.

To view more of David's books:
amazon.com/author/davidleemartin

SpiritLife
Bible School

**Teaching Ordinary People To Walk Every Day
With An Extraordinary God**

An online Bible School designed for people just
like you. Enrol today.

StudyTheBibleNow.com

A KIND REQUEST

Hi there,

David here.

As an independent author it makes a huge difference when I receive reviews and feedback on my books Amazon listings.

If you enjoyed this book, and felt that it offered some value to you, I would be truly honoured if you would be kind enough to take one moment to jump back over to Amazon and leave your rating and comments.

Thank you so much, and God bless you!